FISH

First published in Great Britain in 2019
by Hodder and Stoughton Limited

Copyright © Hodder and Stoughton, 2019

All rights reserved

Editor: Victoria Brooker
Produced for Wayland by Dynamo
Written by Pat Jacobs

MIX
Paper from
responsible sources
FSC
www.fsc.org FSC® C104740

HBK ISBN: 978 1 5263 1003 3
PBK ISBN: 978 1 5263 1004 0

10 9 8 7 6 5 4 3 2 1

Wayland, an imprint of
Hachette Children's Group
Part of Hodder and Stoughton
Carmelite House
50 Victoria Embankment
London EC4Y 0DZ

An Hachette UK Company
www.hachette.co.uk
www.hachettechildrens.co.uk

Printed and bound in China

Picture acknowledgements:

All images courtesy of Getty Images iStock apart from: p7 tr Shutterstock,
p23 c Shutterstock

(Key: tr-top right, c-centre)

Every attempt has been made to clear copyright. Should there be any
inadvertent omission, please apply to the publisher for rectification.

The website addresses (URLs) included in this book were
valid at the time of going to press. However, it is possible
that contents or addresses may have changed since
the publication of this book. No responsibility for
any such changes can be accepted by either
the author or the Publisher.

CONTENTS

YOUR FISH
FROM HEAD TO TAIL

Fish were the first vertebrates on the planet. They have been swimming in our seas, lakes and rivers for more than 500 million years and scientists believe there are more than 30,000 different species alive today.

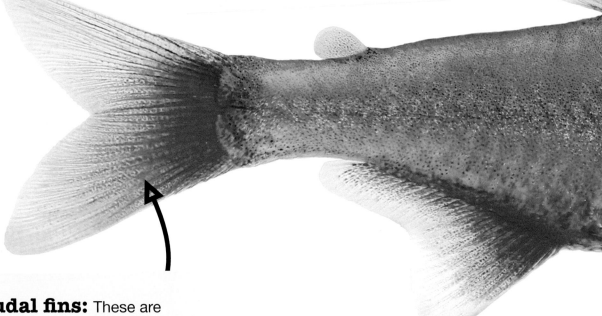

Dorsal fin: This stops a fish rolling over in the water.

Caudal fins: These are also known as tail fins and move the fish forwards.

Anal fin: This keeps a fish stable as it swims.

Pelvic fins: These are found on each side of the fish and help it to turn and to move up and down.

Lateral line: The lateral line is a row of sensors along a fish's side that detect the position of objects, water pressure and vibrations from predators and prey.

Brain: Fish have good memories and can remember routes, people and signals that it's feeding time – sometimes for several years.

Gills: Most fish cannot breathe air so they swallow water and push it out through their gills, which extract oxygen from the water.

FISH FACTS

- Some fish lay eggs and others give birth to live young. Baby fish are often eaten, even by their parents, so they need to be moved to a separate tank if they are to survive.

- Surprisingly, fish can drown! Fish need oxygen and if there's not enough oxygen in the water, they will die.

Pectoral fins: These are where a fish's arms would be (if it had any!).

BEST FISH FOR BEGINNERS

If you're new to fish keeping, it's best to start with freshwater fish. Marine fish can be expensive and a saltwater tank needs more attention. Freshwater fish are hardy creatures and will adapt more easily if conditions aren't perfect.

Bloodfin tetras are peaceful fish that like to swim in schools of at least six. They enjoy a planted tank with plenty of shelter and mix well with other fish. They can jump, so need a tank with a tight-fitting cover.

White cloud mountain minnows are schooling fish that should be kept in groups of eight or more. They like cold water and are easy to keep and breed. Males are smaller and more colourful than females.

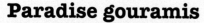

Zebra danios are fast, hardy fish that can survive in a wide range of conditions. They have even been sent into space! They mate for life and are easy to breed. They should be kept in groups of at least six.

Paradise gouramis are a colourful alternative to goldfish. Males often fight so a male and two females is a good mix. They may attack other fish so are best kept alone or with fast fish that can easily escape.

Red shiners are active fish that need a long wide tank and good lighting to display their vibrant colours. They should be kept in groups of at least five, and are fin nippers so need speedy tank mates.

Cherry barbs are peaceful little fish that like tanks with plenty of hiding places. They should be kept in schools of six to ten. Barbs can be fin nippers, so it's best not to keep them with long-finned fish.

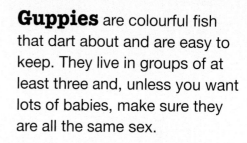

Guppies are colourful fish that dart about and are easy to keep. They live in groups of at least three and, unless you want lots of babies, make sure they are all the same sex.

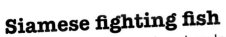

Common goldfish are popular pets, but they belong in ponds because they grow up to 40 cm (16 in) long and can live for more than 25 years. Fancy goldfish are smaller, but they still need big tanks and frequent water changxes because they produce lots of waste. These breeds are slow swimmers, so they shouldn't be kept with other goldfish as they may not get enough food. As goldfish produce a lot of ammonia, they don't mix well with other tank mates either.

Siamese fighting fish are brilliantly coloured and male fish have long, flowing fins. Males will fight, but one male can live with several females. They need warm water and breathe air from the surface.

Swordtails are named after the male's sword-like tail. The best combination is a male and two or more females. They produce live young, but many babies get eaten – often by their own parents.

CHOOSING A HOME FOR YOUR FISH

You'll need to get your tank set up several weeks before bringing your fish home, but it's important to decide what breed of fish you'd like first so you buy the right equipment to suit their needs.

WARM **OR** COLD?

A cold-water tank is easier to set up as you won't need a heater if it's kept in a warm room. Be sure that it's away from sources of heat such as radiators or sunlight so the temperature stays stable. Warm-water tanks allow you to keep a greater range of fish, and many fish are happier and grow better in warmer water, even though they can survive at lower temperatures.

PET CHECK

What you'll need:

- a tank with a well-fitting cover (tetras, barbs and swordtails can jump)
- a light, so you can enjoy your fish at their colourful best
- an air pump to keep the water oxygenated
- a filter system
- gravel or sand
- décor (ornaments and hiding places)
- plants
- a thermometer
- a water-testing kit
- a net
- tank cleaning equipment
- a bucket especially for use with your fish tank
- a heater (if you've decided on a warm-water tank)

TANK SIZE

Check the charts on page 14 and 15 to see how large your fish will grow and then work out the size of aquarium you'll need. The usual rule is 2.5 cm (1 in) of fish to 4.5 litres (1 gal) of water, so you could have five guppies in a 45 litre (10 gal) tank. Some fish like to live in schools, so you'll need space for a group of six or more.

POSITIONING THE TANK

Fish are sensitive to noise, so put the tank somewhere quiet. If you don't have a tank heater, keep your fish in a warm room where the temperature doesn't fall too low at night. A tank full of water is heavy, so it needs strong and stable support, close to an electrical socket.

UNDERSTAND YOUR PET

Don't keep me in a bowl. The water surface is too small so there's not enough oxygen in the water and you can't fit a filter or a heater.

FURNISHING YOUR TANK

Tank decorations and plants don't just make an aquarium more fun for your fish, they also keep the water safe by providing a home for friendly bacteria.

SUBSTRATE

A 5 cm (2 in) layer of sand or gravel on the bottom of the tank creates a natural environment for your underwater pals and helps friendly bacteria grow. Food particles don't usually sink into sand and are removed by the filtering system, but gravel needs regular vacuuming to remove them.

PLANTS

Live plants remove harmful chemicals from the water and provide shelter for fish – they look good too! You can buy special substrates that contain food for the plants' roots. Don't wash the whitish slime off your plants – it's the good bacteria that fish sometimes eat. Just like fish, plants have their own special requirements, so take advice when you buy them.

UNDERSTAND YOUR PET

Don't put too much in the tank or I won't have space to swim around!

DÉCOR

You'll have to wait until your tank is ready before you collect your finny friends, but you can still have fun decorating their new home. Ornaments provide hidey-holes and shelter for shy fish, and they are places for good bacteria to grow.

LIGHTING

Live plants need light to survive, but too much increases the algae in a tank. Start with 12 hours a day and adjust this according to algae growth. If your tank is in a sunny room, you'll only need to switch the light on when it gets darker. LED lights are best because they're cheap to run and don't raise the temperature in your tank.

GETTING READY FOR YOUR FISH

Fish waste, old food and rotting plants all add ammonia to tank water. Ammonia can kill fish, so you need to grow a helpful colony of bacteria to get rid of it. This is called 'cycling' and it takes patience!

A BIT OF CHEMISTRY

Bacteria called nitrosomonas convert ammonia to nitrites. Nitrites are also harmful to fish so you need other bacteria, called nitrobacter, to turn nitrites into nitrates. Aim to get the level of nitrates below 20. A good water-testing kit is essential, so you know when the water is ready for your fish.

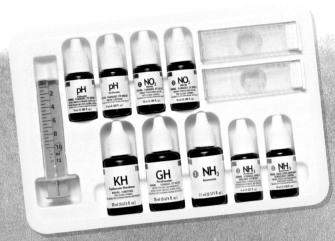

GIVE YOUR BACTERIA A HOME

The friendly bacteria that keep your fish alive live in the substrate (gravel or sand on the floor of the tank), on the tank walls, on any ornaments and in the filter. You should put everything except the fish into the tank at the start of the cycling process.

FILL UP THE TANK

Tap water is best for fish tanks, but you'll need a chlorine remover. Chlorine kills bacteria – including the friendly ones you're trying to encourage! Fill your tank with the dechlorinated water and add two or three teaspoons of household ammonia. Wait for an hour then use your test kit to test the ammonia levels in the water. You are aiming for 3–5 parts per million, so add more if necessary.

TEST, TEST AND TEST AGAIN

After a week, test for nitrites – you should see ammonia going down and nitrites going up. When the ammonia reaches zero, add a teaspoonful each day to feed your bacteria. Nitrites should peak, then fall, during the third or fourth week. Then start testing for nitrates. When the nitrates are climbing and ammonia and nitrites are zero, you should change 60 to 80 per cent of the water to bring the nitrate level to below 20. Leave the tank overnight, then add your fish a few at a time.

TAKE CARE!

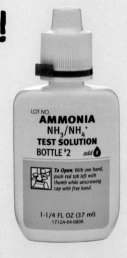

Ammonia is a dangerous chemical so read the instructions carefully or ask someone else to add it to the tank. If you don't want to use ammonia, you can drop some fish flakes into the tank each day until you reach an ammonia reading of 3–5 parts per million.

SPEEDING THINGS UP

Cycling takes up to six weeks! You can speed it up if you have a friend with a healthy tank who can give you some substrate or ornaments already colonised by bacteria – but there's a risk of introducing snails and parasites to your tank. Living plants, such as Vallisneria and Hygrophila, are helpful because they absorb ammonia.

STOCKING YOUR AQUARIUM

Once you've decided to have a cold-water or warm-water tank, it's time to choose your fish. If you want a 'community tank', which is home to different species, you'll need to work out which ones can live together happily.

FINNY FRIENDS

Tanks of mixed fish are fun, but make sure they're all happy at the same temperature and won't attack one another. Fin nippers should never be kept with long-finned fish, and aggressive fish, such as paradise gouramis and Siamese fighting fish, should live with speedy swimmers that can dart for cover. All fish get stressed in overcrowded aquariums so don't overstock your tank!

FISH FOR A COLD WATER TANK

Make sure the temperature in your tank doesn't drop too low at night. Bloodfin tetras, zebra danios and cory catfish need a water temperature of at least 18°C (64°F).

Fish	Adult length	Water temperature	Tank mates
Bloodfin tetra	5–7.5 cm (2–3 in)	18.5–24°C (65–75°F)	Peppered cory catfish
White cloud mountain minnow	2.5–3.8 cm (1–1.5 in)	15.5–23°C (60–73°F)	Peppered cory catfish, zebra danio
Paradise gourami	7.5–12.5 cm (3–5 in)	15.5–24°C (60–75°F)	Zebra danio if there's plenty of space
Zebra danio	6 cm (2 in)	18–24°C (64–74°F)	White cloud mountain minnow
Red shiner	5–10 cm (2–4 in)	15–25°C (59–77°F)	Zebra danio, white cloud mountain minnow
Peppered cory catfish (see page 16)	5–7.5 cm (2–3 in)	18–25°C (64–77°F)	White cloud mountain minnow, bloodfin tetra

HEALTH CHECK

- Fish should be alert and active, and swim in a normal way.

- Avoid any that have cloudy or protruding eyes.

- They should not have any sores, spots or ragged fins.

FISH FOR A HEATED TANK

Some fish that can survive in colder water also do well in a heated tank. Check that the maximum temperature these fish can cope with matches that of your warm-water tank.

Add fish to your tank a few at a time, starting with the hardiest, and keep testing the water.

Fish	Adult length	Water temperature	Tank mates
Cherry barb	5 cm (2 in)	23–27°C (73–81°F)	White cloud mountain minnow, some tetras
Guppy	5 cm (2 in)	18–28°C (64–82°F)	White cloud mountain minnow, some tetras, Kuhli Loach
Swordtail	14 cm (5.5 in)	22–28°C (72–82°F)	Peppered cory catfish, guppy, some tetras
Siamese fighting fish	6.5 cm (2.6 in)	24–30°C (75–86°F)	Peppered cory catfish
Kuhli loach (see page 16)	10 cm (4 in)	25–28°C (77–82°F)	Most fish that are not large enough to eat them

THE CLEAN UP CREW

Algae and snail infestations are common problems, but there's an army of cleaners that will keep them under control. Most fish live in the middle and at the top of the water, so there's room at the bottom for these interesting creatures.

HELPFUL SNAILS

The zebra nerite snail has a beautiful, striped shell and a big appetite for algae. Unlike other algae-eating snails, it won't attack your plants, but you may need to feed it algae wafers from time to time. The assassin snail will help you to get rid of snail pests. If it runs out of snails to prey on, you'll need to feed it meaty foods.

BOTTOM DWELLERS

Cory catfish, such as the peppered cory, help keep tanks clean by eating algae and bits of leftover food. These peaceful bottom-feeders should be kept in groups of at least four and need a sandy substrate so they don't damage their barbels.

Eel-like kuhli loaches are nocturnal and hide during the day. At night, they search for dropped food at the bottom of the tank and in crevices, so filters and pump intakes should be covered with mesh. They need a fine sand substrate because they love to burrow.

UNDERSTAND YOUR PET

Although I'm eating up leftovers, I need feeding too! Make sure you give me food that sinks to the bottom.

SCAVENGER SHRIMP

Red cherry shrimp are scavengers that feed on algae and plant debris, while ghost shrimp clear up any leftover food. They both make peaceful tank mates for fish that are too small to eat them.

ADDING NEW TANK MATES

Rearrange the ornaments in your tank and feed your fish before you introduce newcomers, or territorial fish may attack them. Put the plastic bag holding your new pets into the aquarium and leave it unopened for 10 minutes, so they get used to the temperature.

Open the bag and pour in a cup of tank water, then reseal it and let it float for another 10 minutes. Keep repeating until the bag is full, then use a net to transfer the new tank mates to the aquarium. Don't mix any water from the bag into your tank water to avoid spreading snails or diseases.

FEEDING YOUR FISH

Like all animals, fish need the right food to stay healthy. Some are carnivores and eat other creatures, some are omnivores, and others will eat anything!

DON'T OVERFEED YOUR FISH

In the wild, fish may go for days without finding food and eat whenever they get the chance. Fish that overeat can suffer health problems so giving them a small amount of food once or twice a day should be enough. Any leftover food can block your filter or rot in the tank. If any food is left after 10 minutes, scoop it up with a net and give them a bit less next time.

FEEDING NOCTURNAL FISH AND FRY

Fish that are active at night, such as kuhli loaches and some catfish, should be fed just before you turn the lights off. Baby fish (fry) need special food because normal fish food is too large for them to eat.

CATFISH

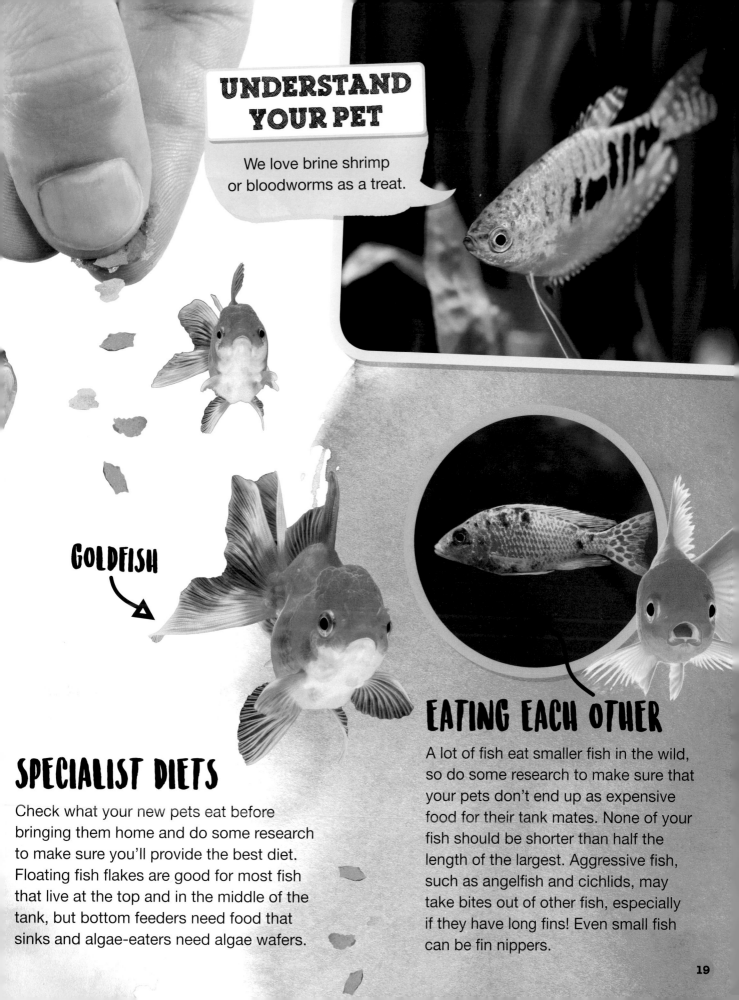

UNDERSTAND YOUR PET

We love brine shrimp or bloodworms as a treat.

GOLDFISH

SPECIALIST DIETS

Check what your new pets eat before bringing them home and do some research to make sure you'll provide the best diet. Floating fish flakes are good for most fish that live at the top and in the middle of the tank, but bottom feeders need food that sinks and algae-eaters need algae wafers.

EATING EACH OTHER

A lot of fish eat smaller fish in the wild, so do some research to make sure that your pets don't end up as expensive food for their tank mates. None of your fish should be shorter than half the length of the largest. Aggressive fish, such as angelfish and cichlids, may take bites out of other fish, especially if they have long fins! Even small fish can be fin nippers.

KEEPING YOUR TANK CLEAN

Good tank maintenance will keep your pets healthy. If there's a build-up of algae, or if food and waste are floating in the water, it's time to take action.

CLEANING THE TANK

Only special tank-cleaning equipment should be used as traces of soap or cleaning products could harm your fish. Get everything ready in advance and prepare the replacement water the day before so it's at the right temperature. Here's what you'll need:

PET CHECK

- algae scrubber and scraper
- gravel vacuum cleaner
- bucket
- replacement water

CLEAN YOUR TANK IN THIS ORDER

- Unplug all electrical items.
- Remove ornaments, but leave live plants in the tank.
- Clean the inside of the glass with an algae scrubber, and a scraper if necessary.
- Twist the gravel vacuum through the gravel. The gravel will drop back into the tank while any debris goes into the bucket with the water. If you have sand instead of gravel, hold the vacuum hose above the surface so it sucks up waste without disturbing the sand.
- Rub algae off the ornaments, then rinse the filter pad and ornaments in the water you removed from the aquarium (don't use tap water).
- Replace the filter pad and ornaments.
- Replace the water you have removed with fresh water.
- Plug everything back in, but leave the tank dark for a while. Tank cleaning is stressful for your underwater friends and the darkness will keep them calm.

WATER CHANGES

Aim to change about 20 per cent of your tank's water each week. Never change it all because you will lose the friendly bacteria that keep it healthy. Don't use water straight from the tap to replace it. If you fill a container the day before, the chlorine will have evaporated and it will be at room temperature. Otherwise use a declorinator. Check the temperature before adding it to your tank.

PESKY SNAILS

Snails or their eggs can be transferred to a tank when fish or plants are added. Most snails don't need a mate to breed, so a single snail can soon become many snails! You can control them by hanging a lettuce leaf on the side of the glass overnight and removing any snails that are attached to it in the morning, or by using a snail trap. Fish such as Siamese fighting fish, and some loaches and catfish, eat snails. Or you could get an assassin snail to do the job!

Assassin snails

LOOKING AFTER YOUR FISH

Fish are not demanding pets but they rely on you to keep them healthy. The best way to avoid problems is to keep the tank clean and quarantine new fish before adding them to your aquarium.

FIN ROT

If a fish has ragged fins it may be suffering from fin rot. This infection is often caused by conditions in the tank such as bad water quality or overcrowding. Make sure none of the fish are nipping others, thoroughly clean the tank, and do a 30 per cent water change. Buy a fin rot treatment and follow the instructions on the bottle. Keep testing the water quality and clean the tank regularly.

ISOLATION TANK

Disease spreads quickly in an aquarium, so it's a good idea to keep a small tank as a hospital for sick fish. You'll need a cover, a heater and a filter, and it's best to keep the filter in the main tank so it's already colonised with good bacteria. A small tank is useful for quarantining new fish before introducing them to the main tank, and for raising fry if your fish breed.

We can't tell you if we feel ill, so please keep a close eye on us.

WHITE SPOT DISEASE (ICH) AND VELVET

Ich and velvet are both caused by parasites on fish's skin. Fish in poor conditions or with a bad diet are most at risk. Take a close look if your fish start scratching themselves on rocks or ornaments. Fish with ich have small white spots that look like sand and those with velvet have gold- or rust-coloured film on their skin. You can buy treatments to kill the parasites.

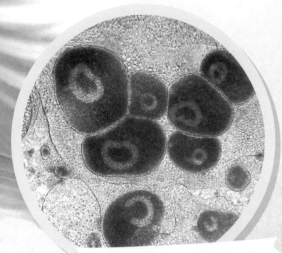

Freshwater fish parasite under microscope

ELECTRICAL SAFETY

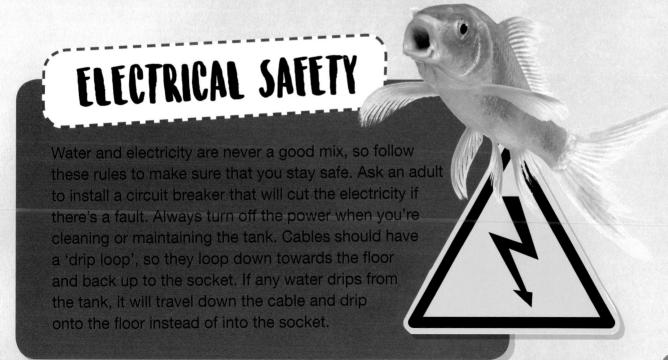

Water and electricity are never a good mix, so follow these rules to make sure that you stay safe. Ask an adult to install a circuit breaker that will cut the electricity if there's a fault. Always turn off the power when you're cleaning or maintaining the tank. Cables should have a 'drip loop', so they loop down towards the floor and back up to the socket. If any water drips from the tank, it will travel down the cable and drip onto the floor instead of into the socket.

UNDERSTANDING YOUR FISH

Watching how your fish behave will give you a good idea how they're feeling. In many cases, unusual behaviour is caused by overcrowding, poor water quality or the wrong tank mates.

HANGING ABOUT AT THE SURFACE

If fish are hungry, or expect food at the same time each day, they might swim up to the surface when someone approaches. Otherwise the water temperature may be too cold lower down the tank, so check the thermometer.

GULPING AIR

Labyrinth fish, including Siamese fighting fish and gouramis, breathe air from the surface because the water in their natural environment is low in oxygen. If other fish seem to be gasping for air you must check whether the tank is dirty, too overcrowded, or if the filter or air pump needs fixing.

SIAMESE FIGHTING FISH

We like to hang out in a gang of at least eight.

BULLYING BEHAVIOUR

If your fish are hiding or chasing others or being chased, they may be stressed. Test the water for ammonia and check that it has enough oxygen. Some fish are naturally aggressive so make sure they have suitable tank mates. If a male fish chases a female he may want to mate with her or, if they have babies, he could become territorial to protect them. If a bottom-feeder doesn't get enough food, it may try to eat the slime coating that protects its tank mates' skin.

PEARL GOURAMI

LONERS AND SHOALERS

Some fish live in shoals or schools. This protects them from predators and they won't be happy unless they're in a group of a certain size. This varies according to species, so check how many you will need. Male fish such as Siamese fighting fish and gouramis will fight rival males and may attack other fish, so should be kept alone or with one or two females.

DIY DÉCOR

You can buy all sorts of ornaments for your tank in a pet store, but why not use your imagination to make some of your own?

DECORATING DOS AND DON'TS

Fish are sensitive to chemicals, so any materials in your tank must be aquarium-safe. Avoid metal objects and anything painted and not sealed. Rocks and driftwood may also affect the water so it's best to avoid them! Make sure there are no sharp edges that may scratch your fish, as injuries can lead to fin rot.

CREATE A COLOURFUL BACKGROUND

Adding a background looks great and also helps the fish that are worried by seeing their reflection in the glass. Print out an image or draw your own to tape to the outside of your tank. Laminate your background or cover it in sticky-back plastic to stop it getting wet!

BRICK BUILDS

Use your imagination to create an underwater world with plastic bricks. You could build a shipwreck, lost city, or a castle for your fish! Make sure the bricks are clean, then soak them in a weak solution of bleach, rinse and leave them to dry. They should no longer smell of bleach.

HOMEMADE HIDEY HOLES

Fish love places for hiding in! You can make a cave by laying a new terracotta plant pot or a coffee mug on its side. Or try carving a door in half a coconut shell, making sure that all edges are smooth. Coconut shells need to be boiled in water for 20 minutes, drained and reboiled three or four times until the water is clear.

FISH QUIZ

By now you should know lots of things about fish.

Test your knowledge by answering these questions:

1 **Where is a fish's caudal fin?**

    a. Under its body

    b. On its tail

    c. On its back

2 **Which of these may nip the fins of long-finned tank mates?**

    a. Red shiners

    b. White cloud mountain minnows

    c. Cory catfish

3 **Why shouldn't you keep fish in a bowl?**

    a. They get dizzy swimming in circles

    b. The surface is too small to provide enough oxygen in the water

    c. They bump into the sides

4 **Which of these chemicals is dangerous for fish?**

    a. Ammonia

    b. Nitrites

    c. Both of these

5 **Why don't zebra danios and kuhli loaches make good tank mates?**

    a. They don't like the same water temperature

    b. The danios will eat the Kuhli loaches

    c. They will fight

6 Small white spots are a sign of which fishy disease?

a. Fin rot
b. Velvet
c. Ich

10 Why might fish be hanging about at the top of the tank?

a. The water is too dirty
b. The water is too cold lower down the tank
c. There is too much algae in the tank

7 Why is the zebra nerite snail a useful tank mate?

a. It eats other snails
b. It eats algae
c. It eats leftover food

8 Why aren't fish flakes the best food for catfish?

a. They float and catfish are bottom-feeders
b. They don't like the taste
c. They only eat meat

9 What should you do when you introduce new fish to the tank?

a. Take all the other fish out of the tank first
b. Empty the bag of water containing the new fish straight into the tank
c. Rearrange the ornaments in the tank

QUIZ ANSWERS

1 **Where is a fish's caudal fin?**

b. On its tail

2 **Which of these may nip the fins of long-finned tank mates?**

a. Red shiners

3 **Why shouldn't you keep fish in a bowl?**

b. The surface is too small to provide enough oxygen in the water

4 **Which of these chemicals is dangerous for fish?**

c. Both of these

5 **Why don't zebra danios and Kuhli loaches make good tank mates?**

a. They don't like the same water temperature

6 **Small white spots are a sign of which fishy disease?**

c. Ich

7 **Why is the zebra nerite snail a useful tank mate?**

b. It eats algae

8 **Why aren't fish flakes the best food for catfish?**

a. Because they float and catfish are bottom-feeders

9 **What should you do when you introduce new fish to the tank?**

c. Rearrange the ornaments in the tank

10 **Why might fish be hanging about at the top of the tank?**

b. The water is too cold lower down the tank

GLOSSARY

algae – Very simple plants that include seaweed. Algae can spoil the look of your tank and harm fish and plants. Too much light and overfeeding both help algae to grow.

ammonia – A chemical that is produced in a fish tank when food, algae and fish poop break down. It can kill fish and plants.

bacteria – Microscopic living things that are found everywhere. Some are dangerous and cause diseases, while others are helpful and keep animals healthy.

barbel – A whisker-like organ that hangs from the mouth of some fish. It often has taste buds.

chlorine – A chemical in tap water that kills bacteria. Leave tap water to stand overnight so the chlorine can evaporate, or use a dechlorinator, before adding it to your tank otherwise you will kill the friendly bacteria.

cycling – Growing a colony of friendly bacteria that will remove ammonia and nitrites from the water in your tank.

dechlorinator – A chemical that removes chlorine from water.

décor – The ornaments and decorations in a fish tank.

freshwater – Water that does not contain salt.

fry – Baby fish.

hardy – Able to survive in difficult conditions.

ich – Short for Ichthyophthirius Multifilis, which means 'fish louse with many children'. Ich is a parasite that burrows into a fish's skin and produces hundreds of babies that quickly spread throughout the tank.

loach – A bottom-feeding freshwater fish.

marine – Found in the sea, or fish that need to live in salt water.

nitrate – Nitrates are produced from nitrites (which can kill fish) by friendly bacteria. Nitrates are less harmful, but levels should be kept below 25 parts per million or fish will suffer.

nitrite – Bacteria called nitrosomonas change dangerous ammonia in tank water to nitrites. Nitrites can still kill fish, so they need to be converted to nitrates by bacteria called nitrobacter.

nitrobacter – Bacteria that change harmful nitrites into nitrates.

nitrosomonas – Bacteria that change ammonia into nitrites.

nocturnal – An animal that sleeps during the day and is active at night.

parasite – An animal that lives in or on another creature and feeds from it (often by sucking its blood).

quarantine – separating an animal from others to stop illness or disease spreading.

school – A group of fish.

shoal – A large number of fish that swim together as a group.

substrate – The material, usually gravel or sand, on the floor of a tank.

velvet – A common disease caused by a tiny parasite. Affected fish are covered by a gold- or rust-coloured dusty film.

vertebrate – An animal with a backbone.

INDEX